Quarter Notes

Quarter Notes

Carroll Blair

Aveon Publishing Company

Copyright © 2012 by Carroll Blair

New Edition

All rights reserved. No part of this book may be reproduced, or transmitted in any form or by any means, electronic or mechanical, including photocopy, recording, or by any information storage or retrieval system without prior permission of the publisher.

ISBN: 978-1-936430-23-9

Library of Congress Control Number
2012920984

Aveon Publishing Co.
P.O. Box 380739
Cambridge, MA 02238-0739 USA

Also by Carroll Blair

Grains of Thought
Facing the Circle
Reel to Real
Shifting Tides
Reaches
Out of Silence
By Rays of Light
Into the Inner Life
Gnosis of the Heart
Soul Reflections
Beneath and Beyond the Surface
Of Courage and Commitment
For Today and Tomorrow
In Meditation
Sightings Along the Journey
Through Desert's Fire
Offerings to Pilgrims
Human Natures
(Of Animal and Spiritual)
Atoms from the Suns of Solitude
Colors of Devotion
Voicings

Contents

Part I

Hymn Say	3
Enter Play	4
Beyond the Spoken	5
Private History	6
Of Love's Descending	7
Count S	8
Bless Them Katherine	9
Balladine	10
Of New Beginnings	11
Hall's Dream	12
Billing Start	13
Now Showing	15
Madman	16
Damn of It All	18
Child of Angry Song	19
Remains	20
Morning Raptures	21
After the Light	22
Mystic Trampoline	23

Part II

A Man Gone Loco	27
Mean Bastard	28
Loose Testimony	29
Here It Comes	30
Vision	31
Final Flight	32
Headline Story of the L. A. Times January 1st 2021	33
Drama Speak	34
Bus Thought	35
Power Play	36
His Greatest Fear	37
Lesson by Lesson	38
Did an Apple Really Fall on Newton's Head?	39
Homage Due	40
Article Red	41
By the Score	42
Words	43
Not Good Enough	44
The Cost	45
Every Artist	46
Naked Alone	47
Point Invisible	48
Certainty's Lead	49
Second – Wonder	50

Part III

What to Say	53
Woman Beautiful	54
Child Treasure	55
Knowledge of the Heart	56
First Time Not	57
Grateful	58
Tribute to a Lady	59
Strange Occurrence	60
Not Only	61
From a Distance	62
Age Five	63
Better Than Gold	64
Early Teens	65
Late Teen Memory	66
What a Man	67
C'est La Vie	68
Delight in the Unexpected	69
Bump of a Day	70
Still Open	71
Insurance & Company	72
In the Dentist Chair	73
Tar Man	75
Glad	76
Not Yet Begun	77
All but This One	78
Lady in Blue	79

Part IV

Dear Truth	83
Behind It All	84
If Possible	85
Nature's Program	86
Two Sides of Forever	87
The Question	88
All That Counts	89
Between the Walls	90
Restless Sure	91
In the Wild World	92
Blind Trust	93
Reflections from the Mall	94
How Known	95
Throughout Life	96
Change of Heart	97
O & L	98
New Blossoming	99
No Words Without	100
Easier Said Than Done	101
Irony	102
Pileup on the Highway of Thought	103
Solo Journey	104
Probing Eyes	105
A Poet's Dream	106
Two Clouds	107
Gift the Rainbow	108
Picture Perfect	109
For Now	110

I

Hymn Say

Coming out of ordinance I am for a time outgoing
and callous in my speech dusting holidays on stilts
for-s-aking needs, force-aching deeds, comparting
arsenals, encouraging winter's flesh to bathe in fires
of snow remembering dreams shapeless in their
origin swift as the blown ash of a wind calling
to an infinite green before twilights exhausting
themselves on passioned waters bending to the
light that binds slowly, that burns tenderly
beside hurried constellations staining the
beaches of the sky pressed to virgin-ed
ceremony not pleased in its must-would-gain,
stretching to a silence through the vast disorder
born in the interval of time's first mendings
parting days off the years of its story echoed
in the frost of a distant spring tuned to the
haunting of its sigh challenging without rest
(no rest) nor blood (yes blood) holding the
mystery of now-forever reaching, signing a
world complete for all who trade their I
for an eye taunting the believers to the
mocking of their faith, daring them
to let their hero have the final say
. . .

Enter Play

Terribly important or terribly wrong
the face of Method stuck on mimed teachings
like lips to a frozen gate breaking standards of
acceptable-un beyond the pale of repent
strict in rhymes of rumination lifting
strife to the goal of rebirth hiding the
mirror that greets the trail of wavering
bliss turning all eyes to a See of Scold
scalding faced red with a kiss.

Beyond the Spoken

Doors forced open menacing to a rampage
sporting crossed stamina steeped in bitter
betrayals icing the feet of prophetic warriors
two x 2 times too delighting in the sublime falling
of bred victims drowning in humilities years
from their assignment boxing the ears of kings
martyred to the reel of the shone, to the riddle of
the final tome moved by sake and circumstance
with calm beyond the spoken

Private History

Lighting down to a whispered plea
the attic holding in history
ground to regions invisible
tracking forensics across the
plains of metaphysical play
casting all bets aside
rounding before a ribbon
strangled by a knot
laid to dust scraping the
heat off shadows at home
with the ghosts they conceal
betting between themselves
measuring sticks by the yard
smashing pictures for the glass
shining like diamonds
placed in the path where
children must walk and
infants crawl to the place of
role and wonder

Of Love's Descending

Of love's descending grave to the touch
crossed between stall and time's recantings
shades of wounding alibis standing down
remembering siege towering above the rage
expanding, weighting rivers of sigh
shadowing lost soldiers mounting on their
banks there for the sake of each for the other
staring loud in fixing gaze, lifting
fear on spears of revenge
stabbing the air with
eyes of blades

Count S

The all-enchanted evenings by all accounts
played their part marched to fickled scenes
beyond the borders of meaning sacked complete
heavy on the woo that held the veil before the
face of Truth sweet and furied, clad in lace of fancy
freeing games of reconcile threatening to reveal
for reasons prepared to keep to themselves

if that's what will please you

Bless Them Katherine

. . . bless the bluestorm, and the windsong, and the
sail holding in its tell, and the sands kissed by a tide
late in its coming bless the bells beating the steeple
and the pilots and children who won't find their way
home, and the lighthouse ancient in its peace and abandon . . .
and when you curl your fingers in shapes of twisted
wings and all things crippled watching the age from
your window and the snow and sunlight falling upon
earth and stone, remember the bliss that struck you down
sparing the rule its mystery and the gift of goal moving
to the center of your soul, going the way of the
iron warriess knowing that what is not will always
be there for you, blessing the heart of Bless.

Balladine

A star named Balladine crossed the waves of a
universe unruly in its tidings of well intentions
soaking the dial frozen in God's hand more
dangerous than an earth idiot with his finger on
the button singing hymns to the blind without
buttons on his sleeves flaunting tattoos of earlobes
sizzling on a wall and flies on a fall near arrows
pointing to a sky for devils left praying mourning
quantities of divine senses condemned to a prophecy
held before the eyes of Job and a portrait of
Just-You-Wait framed to field beyond polar
expanse and catapult-gleam raising the state of
Suddenly to new heights of expectation
rocking the sacred to sleep.

Of New Beginnings

The walls are turning in circles so much to choose from
does it really matter what day it is —

the block is on the sofa —

tangerines are bleeding in the sink —

the Pope's on call-waiting —

Melville's in the kitchen still looking for the eggbeater —

the Klan won't leave the nursery —

does it really matter what time it is

clarities smear the deck with tease waded through by
innocents paying last respects —

Jacob's still roaming the lawn with his ladder —

the garden lies ready to grow —

missionaries draw savages in the dirt sending presidents screaming
to their rooms their pails scarred and empty

does it really matter what day it is   in this day of new beginnings

Hall's Dream

There was shaving, and blood bits, and appearances not kept, beige and rouge and lipstick painting neckties in the shape of napkins covering the bones of a cold knight kept in the oven for ransom — from top to bottom (H)all denounced the rescue launched by a dwarf down on his luck hosting astrologers in his chambers for such an occasion. First the mothers, then the daughters led by the hair their gowns stealing dust from the floor on their way out — (things were never this shy [so hard] when Plato was in charge) — a fire hose outside was ready to blow — kidnappers warmed their cars for the prey on its way eager to assist for the hell of it for the joy of it smuggling scorpions in the rear ready to do their part if the dwarf so ordered . . . the plan going as planned — everything in place for the masked shepherd to make his entrance with eagles on his shoulders and goats tied to his wrists bleating a prelude to Bacchic ceremony soothing to cannibals watching all exits and the jokers signing autographs in the center of it (h)all — and then felled havoc . . . the fruit of wiz-dumb exalting in its feast moved south out of season into a march of Easter-made thieves steering a world to sleep and all who dared to enter without pass or parachute the password to the Dream keeping to itself all secrets and clues to the meaning of it (H)all trapped in Freedom's Hell mapping the parable parade with the bold of blind faces seeding a message unheard unseen yet goes on beating . . .   beating

Billing Start

The deal was made with a handshake and a smile promising
delivery — four carts of joy straight from the bailer's heart
sliced in pairs genial in their forthcomings but for the layers in
hiding shaped more sensibly, matched to the care that will
guard it with nine lives not chosen as yet — waxed mannequins
included — here to please if you please . . . corrections also in-
cluded — a dime lying crooked in the mud placed geniusly
for the jack-in-the-box tagging along going to the block
bouncing steady to the corner of the block — auctioneers
busy in the street sound pictures of escape so defiant in their
ways no one warned of their loathing ready with a civil
disobedient go-screw-yourself-glad-to-be-disrupting-
your-peace attitude to all but the pawnbroker insisting
everything will be o k . . . o.k.   O.K. so you
weren't dealing with a full deck when making
the deal to change your life for the better
making peace with Illusion bringing its
loaded dice to the table brilliant in its fat
chance turning before the eyes of innocents
ready to believe anything stuffed with riddles
wanting to scold in their look - here - comes -
the - bride deceits champagneing your ambitions
stored stories high in a marginally clad dream
forcing comfort to your heart by the sale
of a life moving along for a keeper's sake
the hope that refuses to die — a first glance

was not what you had in mind pelted with
sinned attacks cursing your every move
poor gullible fool promising a world
before its start   Better pack your bags and
take the next flight to Nowhere circle the globe if need be
circle it for eternity like a Russian cosmonaut whose nose
no longer bleeds and is frightened no more by the face of death
the blue jewel no longer seen shining out of place spinning in the
black void housing a world of lunatics   yes go now move
quickly — your family's been told and all who'd care to know
you're going on a business trip the mad business of saving your
soul or at least taking it for repairs — sharpshooters will be
waiting for you we'll do what we can to distract them
lure them away from killing your only chance to do something
worth a while   Don't forget to trust your instincts (there's really
nothing else) they'll always do right by you (no matter what
you do) — Go now, quickly, and take your armchair with you.

Now Showing

Jumping from one concentration to another by the
seat of his pants by the orders of a trance
the captain demanding attentions beyond the call of Truly
amazed at the intensity of resolve shooting two pigs
in a blanket (one crime fits all) — a riverboat bride
was ready to receive her earnings — cost essential
to the catalogued crew bringing things together
for all but the rabbits set for the stew —
satisfaction guaranteed for someone or at least
something like the gadfly on the waters below
(make that muddy waters) and the sun playing
peekaboo through the clouds with passengers
bidding farewell to the captain preparing for his fate
cleaning his whistle for the major blow
waiting for the cry of mankind overbored
proud (so proud) to be part of the show.

Madman

What can you tell us about the light flickering in your head
and the vision corresponding to the crucified in your eyes
and the bowl of Quiet Please sitting proudly on your table
sounding silent in the dark and the cuckoo in your clock
refusing to come out and the minute hand tracking the
hour past its hour and the soon coming into view and
the dream partial to the laws of rejuvenation and the
razor splitting letters in the soup and the telltale
registering ten to the power of a sneeze
and that page from your diary

Ha　　Ha　　Ha　　Ha　　Ha

Ha Ha　　Ha　　Ha　　　　Ha Ha Ha

Ha Ha Ha Ha

Ha　Ha　Ha　Ha　Ha　Ha

& Ha　& Ha　& Ha　& Ha　Ha　Ha

Ha Ha Ha Ha Ha Ha Ha Ha Ha Ha Ha Ha

Ha　　　Ha　　　Ha　　　Ha

Ha　Ha　Ha　Ha　　Ha　　Ha　　Ahhhh

and the feigning of ways panting like a Sumo parade
ground in figures of speech and the words pale as a rosary of

white beads and the fame dropping the frame of its glory
and the elements turning on themselves, the passions
killing themselves the heart preparing a soil of New to
suffer, to grow, to love, to bear fruit and one day
tell us dear madman about the worlds turning in the
depths of your soul and the truths spilling out of there
into that something the angels call life.

Damn of It All

Down it all to the damn — damn — damn of it all
censoring radicals in a mainstream of much to do
about nothing *nothing at all to do with it*
to do with you or so you say you say
you curse the day you were born
(no not the day just the hour)
committed to a loathing no truth
could ever escape lost in a yearning
for yearning's end baiting miracles
not concerned with themselves with
the details of understanding themselves
forcing questions into a box ready to be
shipped to the ends of the earth
out of the way like a maiden left
in the woods to birth her bastard
bleeding before the dawn daring a world
to wake daring it to look, to see (w)hol(l)y
through the damn   damn   damn of it all

Child of Angry Song

Into a path of triumph you cast in future bond
oh child of angry song
visiting places of conspiracy
anchoring the must that allows them to be
locked in trust of sayings
cold beside the living
folding grades of promise in your hands
piercing the envelope in which you must place them
sensing your time has arrived
sworn to ruled rejection
turning to whispers freed from the rage
missing the headline on the way to your battlefield
Hope Gives Birth To Twins   not known if
they will survive born on a battlefield
. . . .   your battlefield

Remains

gathering clues of images worn through spells
volatile in their wake preparing for plays of
geared perfection charged before the raid
rising without shadow attracting secrets
keen to juvenile perspective blighting terror
in gales of nonchalance stunting the wave of
reflection set to grave multiples growing by
scents of disbelief, plunging untraceable
into the mole of Sumwhere to Aum . . .

Morning Raptures

leased for a stroll down future lane signing the
floor of Fate in white the walls and curtains black
splitting down the middle reminding as the Swan song
sung most dutifully as its murderer waits on deck
betraying even numbers balancing force by scale
of coarse through course of mime-filled thunder

After the Light

Gone to the trials of everlasting birth, of
ever fading death; stern to the blackness
surging toward the light dancing in the nude
without fear, without hope, without sin;
all for a search, the search for phantom's gold
cradled in the tides of eternals blessed;
Love denying refusal, refusing denial
to the end of nether-time falling to all
but the angel of Falling, never to be
heard from again

Mystic Trampoline

. . . may the eye of Science drop in your lap
catching you flush in your cynical phase
sending worlds to their graves before they are born
and pierce the minds of neophytes deep with
slivers from Life's shattered mirror picking
illusions between the cracks promised to
goals unsealed (yes) craving bold testaments
from prophets raised to fire, your bouncing
secrets cutting holes in the face of God's smile
come to here forsaking nowhere . . .

II

A Man Gone Loco

A man gone loco looking for a night to tease
looks shabby the chances of finding the right one
the boiler room's ready to explode *no not explode*
just boil a little anger to steam about nothing
or maybe something really big in its broad manner
of haste I mean pacing around the sofa looking for
kangaroo hairs while a neighbor rings the doorbell
asking you out to play the night not looking right
(i.e. chances of finding the right one) [i.e. to tease]
or maybe it's the neighbor who's not right I mean
in his own aerial way but no way can I go
anywhere with *him* though not a clue to the reason
for apprehension, for the hesitation don't really
need one to follow the beat swinging in double time
single all the way following solo intuition into the
realm of serial maze drawn to the outer inn of
inner world pitching tales of lost time sealed in
passports hidden in the minds of mad clerks
seeing camels to the river-riding so inviting
in its chill and flow, think I'll go — yes let's go
! the banks will support us, cover our feet with
mud and moonlight perhaps move us to dance a
little jig or something larger out into the
go-cold starry night, now calling to yet
hiding from the man gone loco

Mean Bastard

He knows what it means to be mean
the mean bastard standing at the corner of
Mean Street folding papers in his hands
crushing cigars between his teeth
scolding the world with piercing eyes
the world not cruel enough not mean
enough for his liking like the like the
story of taking candy from a baby
not good enough (i.e. mean enough)
should also take its carriage
so he preaches so he teaches
the mean bastard standing on the
corner of Mean Street looking for
someone to squeezefleecebleed

Loose Testimony

A loose testimony shaped in a figure eight
prowled about a house of commons looking
for prayer books to feed on — the cat
led it to its desired prey — the testimony
repaid him by stealing his milk . . .

Lord hear our prayers

Here It Comes . . .

a thought running for its life
being chased by another
and that other by another
running toward the portal of
consciousness zapped like flies
hitting an electric field
thoughts never to be, never
to see the day of night
destroyed before the light

Vision

Devils chasing the chosen blowtorching their rears
laughing behind them all the way, from the time they
leave their cradle to the time they reach their grave
laughing and torching all the way

Final Flight

A mosquito had the misfortune of flying
onto the page of a volume of poetry a
poet was reading hitting the page just as
the poet was shutting the book
closing the book on its life
the mosquito murdered by a poem
and a poet —

they say that's not what poetry's about . . .

some would disagree

Headline Story of the L. A. Times January 1st 2021

God committed suicide at three o'clock this morning —
shot Himself dead in the street with Triumph
tattooed to his forehead and FINALLY
painted on His feet . . . a note was found in
His pocket explaining how He tried to wean
man from Him for years — decades — centuries,
but man, too stupid to take the hint or too
cowardly to take over the lead, left Him no choice
but to do Himself what needed to be done, taking
His life at three a.m. Pacific time in the middle of
Sunset Boulevard on this first day of January
in the year of Our Lord 2021

Drama Speak

Arriving late at the scene two tow trucks crash into each other hurrying to be included in the aftermath of a tragedy . . . bodies lying in the road, the road so cold so very cold, troopers lighting flares sizzling "Traffic Beware." A second's lapse of concentration or one drink too many and Drama's tragic quarter is summoned to work ["must touch as many lives as I can"]. Let's tie this up in a hurry — got other places to go, other lives to meet . . . a house will start burning shortly across the river where people will die then there's the explosion in the chemical plant that will occur soon after that, and the train wreck at 72 mph soon after (can't miss that) to say nothing of the catastrophes happening simultaneously where you'd think I couldn't be present but (guess what) I'm omnipresent! There at every tragedy, at every dire event setting life on its heels and sometimes on its back working without a break in place after place but I must hurry, still hurry, the night is young but so much to do, yes, much to be done, the mayhem never missing a day, skipping never a beat . . . and be sure, all of you, some day in some way I'll touch your life too, for as old as I am and as long as I've been I shall remain forever young, because my work wherever it may be, has only just begun

Bus Thought

What would happen if the life inside everyone's
head on this bus filled to the max jumped out and
started dancing or fighting or laughing or crying
in the aisle or doing a thousand other things
out of place or unsettling that humans are capable
of doing engaging in a play of madness in relation to
one another to rattle or frighten the passengers
ever far from the next stop, the driver looking
straight ahead whistling a flat turn of Dixie watching
the road through the wipers squeaking through the
rain driving for hours never reaching a destination
the gas gauge never moving, the passengers never
ceasing to do the thing most unbearable to the one
closest to them no one raising a whisper to bring
the nightmare to a halt, a slice of Reality's Dream
recalling Sartre's line "Hell is other people"
making damn sure his sentiment was right

Power Play

like Caesar coming in by Cesarean
licking the knife, saving his cry for the throne

His Greatest Fear

A brush with fire (spiritual fire) leaving courage
to fend for itself fleeing as fast as he can away
from himself, he is in panic he is in danger of
meeting himself — a dwarf trotting about in
giant's shoes stumping the toes of an ego
blind without brain without heart
roaming in a dark now rising to the light
about to be exposed (!) oh horrible horrible
(What's Hamlet doing here)

To be singed by spiritual fire . . .
the bourgeois' greatest fear

Lesson by Lesson

A. "I wish to draw your attention to the frail bird pecking away at a leaf that has already been destroyed by a worm coming from an apple that is now inedible." "What do you see?"

B. "A frail bird pecking away at a leaf that has already b.."

A. "No! No! I want to know what *you* see."

B. "(We see) a frail man pecking away at a pretension that has many times been expressed by a fear coming from a heart that is now weighing heavily on our nerves becoming intolerable to our minds moving us to close our eyes and hide our ears from what he has to say but

A. "Class dismissed."

B. we love him just the same."

Did an Apple Really Fall on Newton's Head?

Did an apple really fall on Newton's head? If so,
did he take it home to gaze at and perhaps admire
before it rotted, reflecting on the gift? Or did he
eat it, it later becoming part of his waste? Or did
he leave it lying on the ground after it bounced
from his head left to shrivel and rot, or be pecked
to its seeds by birds or carted off by ants, or left
to the feasting of worms?
This object/inspiration of one-in-a-billion revelation —

(If such a thing did happen)

Homage Due

Every day people pass by libraries in varying strides
passing without notice or show of awareness of just
what it is they are passing by . . . should there not be
some sign of reverence made as many do make when
passing a church or house of worship considering the
works of wonder it holds, the history of humankind's
finest minds, the most magnificent flights of the imagination
there preserved for all of human time — lords of
culture and civilization living on in its chambers
surely there should be some gesture of respect or
homage paid at least in silence when passing a library
where people around the world pass daily by the
millions, some fast on their way to worship

Article Red

Following the reading of an article by a bourgeois
psychiatrist about what he deemed to be the personality
disorders of a rebel-genius a man with a touch of genius
and more than a touch of rebel was moved to muse on
how audacious he thought this was, thinking also of
how common such things are and are likely to
always be — a fleeting mediocrity commenting on the
nature of one whose work will live for centuries . . .
the chump taking it upon himself to shine some light
into the soul of one who wasn't perfect but gave
the world marvels of beauty, indeed gave his life for
his work, paid for it with his blood (isn't that what the
saints do?), this giftless-ordinary presuming to criticize
one whom he will never come close to, not fit to shine
his shoes but oh how common, how very common are
such effronteries, is such arrogance and irreverence
from common surface-life fools . . .

so he mused

By the Score

So many scholars kissing ass so much ass
asses of the living and asses of the dead
holding firm the pedestals on which their idols stand
face face-level to rump dividing their story between
tenure and their masters' glory oh so much to say
(they say) to see, the same sad story the same old sorry
the graying of hair the reddening of eyes disappearing
into yellow pages their own thoughts if ever present
now fading now yellowing as well, slaves to the dreams
of others who dared to be what they could be,
spirits of the highest and less than highest worth
yet all more noble and worthy than they who
dot the i's and cross the t's and
sign their names with Ph.D.

Words

powering
themselves
against the
winds and
rains of
thought
doing their
best
to
hold
their
own
in a
game
they
can not
win —

(They *must* keep up appearances —)

Not Good Enough

The best we've got isn't looking like much these days . . .
consider the fifth century BC had Plato, Buddha, Confucius
and Socrates — the Renaissance had Michelangelo and
Leonardo, and the Age of Enlightenment bore more than a
few whose legacy will inspire forever . . . the nineteenth
century gave the world giants in all disciplines too numerous
to here mention; and yes, it is true, the twentieth century
can boast of Einstein, Ghandi, Picasso and King, and other
titans of achievement who could match with the best of
them, but today; I mean, *today* . . . is there anyone who
could really stand equal to the greatest spirits of the past?
If so, please step forward and make yourself known —
The world's in desperate need of you

The Cost

Man: "More light!"

Life: "More pain!"

Every Artist

knows well that not every comfort is to be enjoyed . . .

some are to be   survived

Naked Alone

Standing naked, solitary, barren of all but its wood
and bark beneath a sky graying to dark telling the
night of seasons is drawing near . . . birds fly by
without stopping to rest upon its branches;
no company from earth or sky, nothing from the
world of wild will be drawn to it this day . . .
a scene almost desperate in its solitude; the
sky's cold indifference adding to the lonely
sight of a tree standing naked and alone . . .

more like man than he would like to believe

Point Invisible

Going out on a limb can sometimes be risky business . . .
some limbs more dangerous than others, more than the
limb-braver bargained for, getting himself stuck beyond
a certain point the invisible point of no return finding it
impossible to move as if he had glue on the soles of his shoes
impossible to turn, to go back, trapped in the middle of his
quest anxiously trying to keep balance, but balance is out of
reach yet one doesn't fall, just strives to steady himself without
pause trying to regain the equilibrium of a life to no avail, a
balance forever lost — a high wire act never wanted, not ever
imagined, the cost never assessed prior to the stretch . . .
the price of going out on that limb

Certainty's Lead

like in those moments when you feel most in charge
everything going the way you want it to the way you
feel it should, moving near the top of the world and
something grabs you from behind, latches on to the
back of your soul something like invisible hands
saying with its grasp 'don't kid yourself fool
 . . . .   don't kid yourself '

Second — Wonder

One second missing from your life just one
and your whole life from that moment on
(yes whole) would be different [surely different]
and not only your life, no — but the lives of all
who are close to you, i.e. who are in your life or
have something to do with your life, and not only
their lives, but the lives of those who are close
to them whom you know nothing about and
the lives of those who are close to the lives
of those who have something to do with them
whom they know nothing about etc. etc.
and the same phenomenon would result
(but not the same result) if just one second
of your life were different, everything
following that second would be different
and the difference affecting the lives of others,
making their lives in some way different
makes you wonder about matters of choice,
of fate, of destiny, of the incredibly subtle
but profound influence that we have on the
lives of others and others in turn on ours
reaching beyond what the mind can see
makes you wonder

one wonder indeed

III

What to Say

I know — I know — . . . you wanted to tell me how much
you liked me but I did something to bruise your sentiment
scattering your words formed in a line preparing to deliver
a message now retreating back into a chamber of your mind
to quickly regroup and deliver a message more safe (yes)
far more benign . . .   something like   I love you

Woman Beautiful

Standing on the boulevard next to the railing
leaning on, now over it, the sea wind gently
lifting her dress caressing more than the eye
can see . . . where the wind is able to go
enough at times (like now) to fill a man
with envy

Child Treasure

I watch a child picking seashells
from the shore carefully placing them
in his little red pail

to him they are worth more than diamonds and gold —

they were to me too

Knowledge of the Heart

No words to describe his joy upon hearing his
child's first word — something he wanted to do,
he wanted to say, but no words to him came . . .
if so, the event would be less precious, more   so so . . .

something the heart well knows

First Time Not

Arriving home wearing a frown upon his face weary in both
body and mind making his way to his favorite chair sitting
himself down his young daughter then climbs on his lap
asking, "What's the matter Papa, and what happened to
your thumb all black and blue, ooo big boo boo . . ."
"I missed the nail and hit my thumb" he replies —
not the first time he failed to hit the nail on the head
nor will it be the last, in his work, in his life and in the life
of his child so adoring now sitting on her father's lap
touching gently his bruised hand, forgetting to tell him
her day's stories wishing the pain to go away

Grateful

for the life you have saved held literally in your
hands just days ago now making your rounds
probing the measure of your work asking questions
critical to your examination the patient speaking
clearly her reply now well on her way to recovery
a life you held in your hands that could have easily
slipped away, your calmless energy expected, your
slight aloofness accepted for the life you have saved

I [we] forever in your debt

Tribute to a Lady

To a statue I wake every morning standing on the
back of a lawn two yards away from my window;
a statue of Mother Mary placed in a shrine of exceptional elegance emanating something of grace.
I once saw her up to her heart in snow; never
did she look more serene, more beautiful . . .
Once I brought her flowers and laid them at
her feet and saw them still there the next day
and thought to myself, this lady's o.k. to
accept a gift from one who questions the hype
surrounding her and her son. I catch myself
thinking of her at odd times and places, far from
the hour of dawn and the place where she's
always standing giving me, I must admit,
some welcomed pleasure . . . a piece of comfort.

I've come to appreciate this first sight of the day
of a special lady two yards away, and muse with
amusement joined with affection how we can exist
so close together, this statue that never moves
that has come to move me.

Strange Occurrence

It was imperative to take the medicine every six hours
prescribed for one day only; the first dose taken at 3:00
p.m. taken at this time without thought — no alarm set
for the 3:00 a.m. swallow, the matter important enough
to slip the mind but no matter — the phone rang at
precisely 2:59 a.m. waking me from a sound sleep
the sound of the phone sending a shiver through me
thinking it must be an emergency, that no one
would ever call at this time unless it was (right?) —
charging to the phone I picked up the receiver saying
hello but received no reply though someone is on
the line . . . through the silence I sense a presence
for the twenty or so seconds before hanging up.
Starting to feel anger for being abtuptly awakened
I realized what time it was and what I was supposed
to be doing, the coincidence too strange to be a
coincidence — how could it be . . . that the phone
would ring at this particular time a minute before
the needed medicinal chore . . . strange enough to
raise the question in my mind if only for a moment:
"God, was that you?"

Not Only

Not only do I admire the fly's ability to fly
but also its ability to walk upside down
moving across the ceiling and down the wall
then back up to the ceiling then pausing
for a moment, now more than a moment
suspending itself above me as if to say,
"You see, oh human being, there are things I
can do that you cannot, things that are beyond
you, that are above you, as I am now on the
ceiling standing above you [and upside down
no less (!)]" — This fly possessing gifts that I
and all human beings do not, be they
genius or fool, saint or sot.

From a Distance

From a distance I saw a white cloth breezing between
two branches of a tree tall and shady thinking at first
it was a cat — drawing closer I discovered it wasn't
what I believed it to be then thinking of course
it couldn't be, what in the world could I've possibly been
thinking, the object being too high from the ground
for a small feline to dare climb, or so I thought . . .
Days later on the same path I saw a
neighborhood cat ten feet higher than the cloth
staring at me as if he knew my thoughts as if he
wanted to show that he could indeed do what I
thought he couldn't, standing regal on his conquered
branch both of us staring at each other
his stare more intense looking down at me,
me looking up with that mixed feeling of humility and
gratitude for one who has taught me by proving me wrong,
by putting me in my place.

Age Five

That pain in the forehead from the first exposure of
a bright morning sunlight would make me squint my
eyes and wonder why the sun was so mean
(this at the age of five —)

Now I know the sun isn't really mean . . .
just wants to let us know bright and early
who's the boss

Better Than Gold

The moon lit bright upon the speckled trout
lying on the dock after a long battle barely won
away from the grownups heard laughing in the
cottage stationed well on the highland above
the lake where something powerful had just
taken place — the prize splashing furiously
fighting with all its might moments before
now lying still on the evening dock
resting on red-colored beams shining
in the moonlight . . .

to the eyes of a ten-year-old better than gold
glittering in the sun

Early Teens

. . . we liked to hang out in front of the soda shop —
some friends and I on summer nights then romp
around town when the town closed down except for
the bars . . . one night we stopped at the library wall
when minutes later a man staggered up the street
all bloody and beaten known to all present but me
stumbling from side to side but looking more than
mean enough to want another brawl I asked him if
he needed help but he just moved on grabbing my
shoulder to help himself on his way my friends told
me to leave him alone, said he was the town bully
who looked like he got what he deserved, someone
finally gave him his pay . . . he staggered on in the
1:00 a.m. darkness alone blood covering his face, sweat
soaking through his shirt the night so warm and still
turning from the rage in his heart
burning through the silence

Late Teen Memory

Not wanting to be thought a coward for refusing to
fire the rifle the day before to shoot at nothing in the air
he wakes me at 6:00 a.m. the next morning insisting we
go to the field to shoot geese out of the sky with a shotgun . . .
this making him seem more of a coward in my eyes than
he feared he was the day before
that I never thought he
was   before

What a Man

He was the first . . . first to have the honor of entering
her body — a privilege only someone special should
have a right to, even if the she is less than special
(i.e. not so special to him) — especially if that's
all there is to be between them.

He, so proud of his conquest ("I never even kissed her!")
leaving her in a cool autumn field confused and
weeping —

what a man

C'est La Vie

There was a lottery not long ago where a man bet on long odds, bought himself a ticket and won seventy million dollars. They say it was a one in fifty-five million chance of winning. Won fair and square . . . in the confines of the lottery, yes. But if you bring Life into the fairness question it would seem that in order for someone to hit fairly on a one in fifty-five million ticket he or she would have to be a one in fifty-five million human being, a most extraordinary individual, to say the least, and the odds of *that* happening must surely be longer . . . even more remote —

c'est la vie

Delight in the Unexpected

Passing a sub roll over a bowl of soup with pieces of
pretzels stuck to the bottom side of the roll that were
left in the bread dish, pieces I was about to remove
when plunk! into the soup they went . . . pondering
what to do with the now unwanted combo of soup
and pretzel sitting on the table, the idea came to me
that they might taste good together, that perhaps I'd
like this better than the conventional soup and crackers,
and I did . . . I then realized that this is how many discoveries
take place; the unexpected; — something not looked for
or even desired — discoveries both great and small, this
of course being small (with no significance at all); — but I
experienced a slight thrill, a little joy to be able to experience
in a modest way the feeling the scientist has when stumbling
upon something new in his lab, something he likely would've
never found or thought of, handed to him as a gift from
out of the blue — something like a visit from the muse

(but that's another story —)

Bump of a Day

The moment arrived for my turn to order in
a gourmet bagel shop, I asked for a plain bagel
and the clerk recorded the price of my order on
its wrapper with a magic marker, the smell of it
ruining my appetite and before I could speak,
could stop him from doing the mindless deed
he wrapped the bagel in the wrapper with the
ink still wet or surely not yet dry, the smell of
noxious stupidity charging the air as thick as
this clerk marking all the orders with his magic
marker (why do they call it magic?). No one else
seemed to mind, which made me wonder where
their minds were but also where mine was, getting
jolted from my better-than-usual peace-of-mind
day and why I couldn't toss the incident from my
thoughts as easily as tossing the bagel away
into the trash while walking away.

Still Open

waiting for the hood to close . . . been sitting here
now standing watching the mechanic across the street
working on my car interrupted by phone calls and
customers wanting gas and inclinations to procrastination
waiting in this coffee shop for hours was told it
would be a forty-five-minute job — I use this time
to reflect on the way things are and why they are
and how little I'm surprised when nothing turns
out as planned or predicted and how this mechanic
has contributed to my diminishing faith in the
human race (but not life) this diminishing not
known to him surely unknown but if he knew
and knew now what I was thinking, just now
entertaining I'm sure he wouldn't give a damn
perhaps light another cigarette and wipe his
forehead with his hand caked with grease and reach
for his coffee cup while thinking of how to ask
his boss for a raise and if the weatherman was
right about the forecast for tonight and what his
wife will prepare for supper and what his son will
think of him if he misses another of his baseball
games and how to tell me that the job costs
more than he told me it would thinking
nothing of all that I am thinking of,
both of us standing in our lives
sipping in our dreams

Insurance & Company

The insurance company wants its money wants it now, immediately — faithfully paid for years, miss one payment (just one) and they send you threats of possible cancellation of your policy signed by someone you never met nor will ever meet. Should he not be messaged to go to hell with his company, be sent a notice along with the payment warning of the possible cancellation of his soul for all the money he and his company stole — so eager to collect premiums, far less eager to pay claims when rightfully claimed looking to pay the least amount possible as little as they can get away with, lawyers handy just to handle this art of swindling for them, to tip the scales in their favor slant them to their side as far as they're able, bonuses for those who do this well   should they all not go to hell (?) . . . perhaps one day they will. For now, all I can do is pay the bill.

In the Dentist Chair

musing while waiting for the dentist to begin doing some
needed work, his assistant keeping good and quiet company.
(A pleasant looking woman, somewhere in her thirties.)
He's busy. Business is good and he is happy. He's
talking in the hallway to one of his patients. They're
talking about golf. They speak of playing together someday.
They probably never will, but seem to enjoy discussing the
possibility. I wait in the chair as the assistant carefully
arranges the instruments the dentist will need for what is
scheduled to be done. He enters the room and asks me how
I'm doing; he doesn't listen to my reply. The assistant
hands him a syringe and he tells me to open my mouth
without looking at me or noticing that it is already open.
As he injects the anesthetic into my gum he informs her of
how well his son played at his soccer game the day before
proceeding from there while waiting for my lip to numb
to speak of the new country club he is now a member of
and how great its tennis court is and about the movie he
saw last weekend and the one he wants to see the coming
weekend; she forces a smile and tells him, "that's good;
that's nice" trying her best to appear interested, but her eyes
betray something different. She smiles and feigns interest
all the same. (What else can she do? He's the boss.) He looks
at his watch and asks me if my lip is feeling numb. It's not,
but he would like to begin anyway. He has an important
lunch meeting and I seem to be in the way of his getting
to it on time. He waits another minute . . . he's going on

vacation in two weeks; hints at the expense it will cost and the beautiful resort where he and his family will be staying. A last "that's nice" from the assistant.
Then down to the point:
"Is your lip numb?"
"Kinda, but.."
"Drill"
"Yes doctor"
"Open"

"Did I tell you I was planning to go to the Bahamas this winter and maybe . . . .

Tar Man

He pulls up in front of the house at 7:00 a.m. sharp —
diesel fumes coming through the window screen
what better way to wake to the day . . . he's here to
tar the driveway. He leaves his truck running while
talking to a neighbor; another business opportunity
in the making — none can afford to be missed.
His helper who appears to be his son knocks on the
front door asking the landlord to tell all occupants with
cars in the driveway to move them so they can get
started (the landlord forgetting that today's the day
they were coming). I promptly oblige, wanting them
to do their dirty business and leave as soon as possible
so I can get back to my life and they can go elsewhere
filling the air with poison and covering the ground with
tar and talk to neighbors in the hope of returning again
to their neighborhood and rile other people enough to
inspire them (provoke them) to describe something of
their intrusion and how abhorrent it is that earth and air
must suffer so to earn this man his bread.

Glad

to be free of this that I've seen . . . the need, the
compulsion to outdo another; the determination of
one neighbor to show up the other — one adding a
new deck to his home to complement his new
swimming pool, extensions of himself — increasing
his comfort in-your-face style to all residents living
in the vicinity residing within view of his property
then neighbor two orders a cement truck to his
backyard not more than a day after Sam Decker
finishes his project, orders a walkway to be laid to
a patio not yet built but built it will be to show
old Sam he's not top dog not king of the block
taking the Jones' sacrament to new heights and
lows of absurdity . . . and the shame of it all . . .
the shame that neither of them feel as their hammers
pound and drills scream to the summer sky
indifferent to the carnival noising below . . .

Not Yet Begun

Roaring up and down the street showing off his bike
the young teen at it again showing off himself
roaring especially loud past the houses whose
occupants he most wants to impress, wants most to be
seen by, not only seen but also heard, must not
know or ever heard the line stupid parents tell their
children "children are to be seen and not heard"
testosterone coming alive fueling those portions of
the brain beneath the cortex animal-pure
void of anything close to resembling thought, ego
sprouting illusions of importance
the lessons of insignificance not yet begun

and the roar goes on . . .

All but This One

I hear the cry of an infant downstairs coming from
the apartment below; the weekend always free of
such sounds, the grandparents babysitting their
first grandchild Monday through Friday, their
love missing her, fetching her back on Saturday —
their love for her and mine for them worth more
than this distraction and the work that won't be done;
the thoughts and poems chased away

(all away but this one)

Lady in Blue

. . . so there I was, standing on the sidewalk without a
thought to my name and then she walked by, straight into
my sight to the back of my mind turning over items
I didn't know existed — a lady with no name
(of course she has a name but I don't know it — let's
just call her the lady in blue) walked by without
noticing me — and how much greater her appearance
seemed because she didn't turn in my direction —
a stunning profile of beauty and grace inspiring
sensations without effort, simply by being what she
was, arousing more than just sensual feelings
(and how sensual one must be to accomplish that [!])
The lady in blue on her way to the next phase of
her destiny giving me something as she passed that
she never intended, something she never knew she gave . . .
I thank her just the same.

IV

Dear Truth

Blindfolded walking a tightrope above spiritual fire . . .
what the brave and foolish must do to find you
dear Truth waiting with open claws to rip to shreds
those who manage to reach you, whispering your
secrets in their ears as you tear them to pieces

Behind It All

Always something behind it all, something you
can't see, can't quite get at nor think or feel with
clarity — the thought behind the emotion,
the emotion behind the thought, *the* Thought,
the Emotion of a life always present, always
lurking from behind contributing more to a
life's story than anything snared in the net of
consciousness, designing from beginning to end
through life-time never lasting.

If Possible

If one could encapsulate everything happening in all of Existence, capture in the mind's eye everything at once at any time in history or in the present or the future; that is, glimpse all there is, *all of it*, for a very brief moment, *any* moment — no moment would appear any different than another

(i.e., if such things were possible —)

Nature's Program

Prowling for their next meal to sustain themselves so they can breed a new generation to prowl for their sustenance to sustain themselves for the sole purpose of breeding a new generation, rear them for a period of time so they can continue the cycle of prowling feeding breeding for no discernible reason but for the preservation of the species these animals of the wild . . . and man, in his way, like them in many ways doing what he must to carry on like all animals, the sex drive key to the impetus of motivation and behavior, breeding (the act if not the result) never far from conscious mind, forces beyond his knowledge and control prodding him to bring forth a new generation so they can bring forth another with no more visible purpose than the animals who must prowl for their sustenance to sustain themselves so they can breed a new generation and they in turn, another generation and so on and on blindly following Nature's program slave to her will, the human animal no freer from serving her primary mission of species propagation
than the animals of the wild, but man stands back and smiles believing he's not a part of it — that he is above all this . . .

sure he is

Two Sides of Forever

Billions of years of nonexistence then existence for a short time then billions of years of nonexistence some believing (many) that somehow, some way we *must* continue to be in some field or form as individual entities with soul and sentience for all eternity —

but if so, why not existence in those billions of years before?

The Question

All through man's life the question follows him:
"Who are you?"

He sometimes pauses to listen
.... rarely trying to answer

All That Counts

It is all that counts . . . the thoughts of the philosopher,
the words of the poet; beyond counting the ups and
downs of their brethren like no profession can claim,
keeping to the business of dissecting Existence
laying the fruit of their findings and creations on
Humanity's Table where all are invited to dine . . .
where they usually dine alone

Between the Walls

A crowded hall of adults holds
between its walls thousands of
years of life; thousands
of experiences and countless
dreams; but by the interests
and chatter of the guests
you wouldn't know it . . .
would hardly guess

Restless Sure

Every word, motion of body, connection
with the eyes between one human being
and another, extended to one human being
by another looking face to face to faith . . .

the motive behind the motive: the
assurance that they are not alone

In the Wild World

every prey knows well its predators —

not so in the human world

Blind Trust

Oh the damage done every day in this life because
of blind trust — people trusting that people know what
they're doing, doing what they trust themselves to do
believing in their illusions of thorough knowledge,
of absolute competence to the point of convincing
themselves and others that all that they do is sensible
believing their judgments are always sound
that whatever their ideas put into action are sure
to lead to the desired result, as dependable
as four following three, as trustworthy as the
changing of the seasons to say nothing of the
deliberate deceits manifesting in all corners of
the world every minute of the day in a grand
carnival of swindling never ceasing and the amazing
thing (the most frightening thing) is how many never
learn anything from being had time and again, being
as vulnerable to the follies and knaveries of others as
they were the first time they fell victim to the long short-
comings of human knowledge and always scarce supply
of true goodness because of their trusting-blind-frame-of-
mind, easier than thinking for yourself, being on the
lookout with a healthy skepticism a most reasonable one
for the many holes in the common assumption of man's
taken-for-granted competence and integrity.
Holes that blind trust is unable to see.

Reflections from the Mall

Faces proud, certain; most revealing; betraying a
confidence of those who are wearing them that could
only be the manifest of a profound ignorance
blocking out the true nature of naked existence from
these children grown to the illusion of adult; —
certain that their lives have meaning, that life itself
is filled with knowable meaning, sure of their place
in the world never questioning their right to be,
believing in their value, in their significance, now
walking, talking, laughing, going about their
business questioning never beyond the surface,
beyond appearance moving from store to store
to browse or purchase some comfort or fleeting
pleasure, doubt as to who they are or what they're a-
bout as far removed from their field of consciousness
as the understanding of $E = mc^2$ to the mind of a loon.

A sight for sore eyes these humans blind with certainty,
living in the shallow of their lives

How Known

How does one know that the infant crying in its crib
disturbing the household, disrupting the peace of the
adults is not protesting in the only way it can
against the stupidities that are levelled upon it and
will continue to be, even with the best of intentions
even with the greatest of love (or thought to be love)
by the large ones now taken out of themselves to
tend to the little one wailing in its crib, they without
a clue of what it wants much less what it needs,
though they do believe they know . . .

    indeed   (indeed)

Throughout Life

There are parts of the human soul that tease one
throughout one's life dancing around him,
around her like teasing children saying with
taunt and laughter, "Catch us if you can!"

Or if you dare . . . .

Change of Heart

On the ground lying alone beneath the branch
from which it has fallen, a last gift of fruit
not moved by a wind feeling as though it belongs to
the next season biting the nose and thoughts of one
eyeing the gift tempted to claim it for himself.
Leaves and earth blow around them before making
their way to faraway, beyond the sight of one soon
to turn away from the object of his temptation
deciding not to take it thinking that it would be
like stealing a child from its mother; and how
could he contemplate doing such a thing; — to
steal the only surviving child though soon to die
from its mother now so naked and lonely

O & L

Love's throat gasping at the moment of orgasm
refusing all pretensions of O having something to do with L

but do tell of the one created from two, loved from here
to the break of fear to the ends of kingdom come
coming from O having zero to do with L

oh   do tell

New Blossoming

Wounds healing over in the spirit,
in the heart — something new is
blossoming — something useful,
something unusual . . .

a guess, a hope

. . . this flowering of new pains
with pearls in their teeth

No Words Without

For a few words that rattle the soul of Life,
just a few — what it costs the mind from which
they spring and the life that it commands . . .
no such words come forth sequenced in thought
without blood, spiritual blood . . . or passion
and vision and pain and rage and love

Easier Said Than Done

If we could only correct our errors
could right our wrongs, even a few
(oh just one!) what a blessing it
would be . . . But would it?
To correct anything from the past
would be to turn our destiny another
way in another direction from that
point onward, and the destiny of others
as well — those who pass in and out
of our orbit (i.e. our lives).
Who knows, who can say what other
blunders would be committed by the
correction of just one committed?
Or how many blessings lost?
Best to leave our past in the graveyard
where it belongs and journey into the future
without regret, with a notion if not belief
that all that has gone before was meant to be,
is just Is, is just Was . . . the past no more,
forever gone with only today and
tomorrow to be lost or won.

This [of course] easier said than done

Irony

People torturing themselves trying to get at
thousands of points of thousands of different
things per se when life itself has no point,
just goes from day to day

Pileup on the Highway of Thought

Abstractions crashing into each other . . .
head-on collisions smashing the whole
world of metaphysical mind into
f-r-a-g-m-e-n-t-e-d pieces —

God in a policeman's uniform directing traffic

Solo Journey

I go on by myself in search of myself

and find along the way

demons whispering "that-a-way . . . that-a-way . . ."

all pointing in different directions

Probing Eyes

stirring the hand to jealousy

grasping things with depth and speed

the hand can only dream of

A Poet's Dream

Watching a language
with all its words
tossed in the air
falling at random
then diving into them like
a pile of leaves
rolling in childlike ecstasy
beneath a sun
burning shiny and new

Two Clouds

side by side passing above
in shapes of whales white
floating beautiful through the sky

Gift the Rainbow

What a gift the rainbow is
after a rain has fallen, arching
the sky in beams of color
as if sent by the gods for
any inconvenience the rain
may have caused . . . a sky
of gray just minutes before
pouring and trembling with
thunder, now a picture
of beauty and peace, a
gift indeed . . .   a wonder

Picture Perfect

A flock of swallows landing in a field
hundreds of them touching the ground
simultaneously as if programmed to
synchronization by some cryptical
instruction moving to choreography
one with the other departing
almost as quickly the flutter of
their wings stirring foliage rising to
the wind as they speed to the sky
circling the grounds before
taking their leave in grace-filled
harmony signing the moment with
presence never to be again

not in *this* way   again

For Now

Just here, now, we in pure being, leaving all
thought behind of thought wooing Sensation
from its cave dancing beautifully before us . . .
Is this how those skyborne creatures take flight
on wings of abandoned bliss caring nothing
for what was or will be, the blessing of
present existence keeping them from that
torment, being without care playing their part
in the august venture forever pristine yet old
as it is new, untamed in its play to perfection
guiding through the vast discard, present
without beginning or end . . . The morning
so rich with invitation; what is there to do
but step to the sunrise never looking back
shedding fear after fear as we move forward
cleaving to only the dream that will take us
beyond ourselves and finally, to ourselves,
touching the moment as it fades away
delivering us to the next, resisting nothing,
yielding to the perennial flow of time
turning in the now forever in the Now,
sharing in the eternal magic, in the grand
forever-dance at its calmest yet most
intense, being in the center of all there
is . . . in the all of Everything . . . in the
everything of All

ABOUT THE AUTHOR

Carroll Blair is an award-winning author of more than twenty books. His work has been well endorsed and commendably reviewed, as illustrated by the following commentary from Midwest Review, which proclaimed, *"The poetic expression of Carroll Blair is both unique and compelling. Using word images like the strokes of a painter's brush, Blair creates a resonating recognition that is the mark of a master poet."* He is an alumnus of the Boston Conservatory and lives in Massachusetts.